Open Sesame

June 2016

Ben Freeman Jr.

Scripture verses depicting KJV, NASB and NLT are taken from the E-Sword Copyright 2000-2014, Rick Meyers www.e-sword.net/support.html. All Rights Reserved.
&
Bible Explorer 4.0, Copyright 2006, WORDsearch http://.bible-explorer.com. All Rights Reserved.
Open Sesame
Copyright © 2016 by Ben Freeman Jr.
www.greatlineage.com   ben@greatlineage.com

ISBN 978-0-9977029-6-5
Library of Congress Control Number 2016943480

Published by
Rapier Publishing Company
260 W. Main Street, Suite #1
Dothan, Alabama 36301

www.rapierpublishing.com

Printed in the United States of America. All rights reserved under the International Copyright Law. Contents and/or cover may not be reproduced in whole or in part in any form without the consent of the Publisher or Author.

Book Cover Design: Garrett Myers/ Book Layout: Rapture Graphics.
The views expressed in this work are solely those of the author and do not necessarily reflect the views of the publisher, and the publisher hereby disclaims any responsibility for them. Any people depicted in the imagery provided by the illustrator are models, and such illustrations or art are being used for illustrative purposes only. Illustrations are created by Garrett Myers and the Author, Ben Freeman.
Visit Garrett at garrettmyersart@gmail.com.

Dedication

I am dedicating "Open Ses·a·me" to the dedicated men and women who desire to have a life long relationship with their spouse and not the "Ole Roll of the Dice Relationship" that has become so common in today's world. My prayer is that this book blesses and encourages you, the reader, to continue to strive for the relationship you desire to have with the one you love.

To you, from me,

God Bless

"But you, dear friends, must build each other up in your most holy faith, pray in the power of the Holy Spirit, and await the mercy of our Lord Jesus Christ, who will bring you eternal life. In this way, you will keep yourselves safe in God's love. And you must show mercy to those whose faith is wavering. Rescue others by snatching them from the flames of judgment. Show mercy to still others, but do so with great caution, hating the sins that contaminate their lives."

Jude 1:20-23 (NLT)

Table of Contents

Introduction..7
1. Calling You Fix-It.....................................11
2. Love That Comes First............................17
3. Love Me for Me..23
4. The Bottle..31
5. Comparison...39
6. Couples..43
7. Need or Greed...51
8. Distracted..59
9. Pride & Ego...67
10. Foundations..71
11. Intentions..79
12. The Boxing Ring.....................................85

Short Stories
13. The Dog..93
14. The Thought-of Effect............................97
15. Imaginary Problems..............................101
16. Face to Face..105
17. Stop Repenting and Repent..................109

Conclusion...113

The Introduction

Welcome to Open Ses·a·me. A book for individuals who have a desire to make their relationship with their mate or future mate work. It's for those individuals who desire to say to someone, "Look In·to·me and find the treasure that lies within me." Open Ses·a·me is a book designed to assist you in accessing and unlocking the hidden doors in your relationships. The hidden doors that I will be referring to are hidden hurts, fears, secrets, or goals that only you as a spouse should have access to open.

Open Ses·a·me is a book that will challenge the reader to be honest, open-minded, and open-hearted. We can find a lot of truth from the world's viewpoint on men and women, but there's also a lot a truth that can be found within ourselves as well. That's why in Open Ses·a·me, I'm sharing real life experiences that my wife and I encountered that I believe will be familiar and beneficial to you the reader.

To get a good taste on how Open Ses·a·me will flow, let's begin with these two simple questions.

1. Do you believe someone can love you if they don't know how to love themselves?
2. Do you believe that someone can take care of you if they don't know how to take care of themselves?

In Mark 12:31 it says, "Thou shalt love thy neighbor as thyself." This Bible verse is extremely important to all Believers, and it's important to those who are in serious relationships because without it the relationship may end up in failure.

To me, as a married man, this verse is the glue that can hold and keep couples in relationships together longer. It can help us be happier, which will make our love to grow and evolve over time. That's why we must understand that we must FIRST love ourselves to love someone else.

Have you ever heard the saying *"Real Recognizes Real?"* What this phrase means is that if you are true to who you are, what you like, and how you feel, you will recognize it on others. You will also be able to recognize when someone is "putting on" and not being themselves. It's very important for people in relationships to know how to love themselves before they love another person. Why? Because if you don't know how to love yourself, how can you give your spouse the love he or she need or desire from you if you can't recognize when their happy or not with what you're doing for them? This may not be a familiar way of thinking because of what many of us were taught as children and in church, and that is, "It's better to give than to receive." However a great man once told me, "You must first be a good receiver before you can become a good giver."

When someone knows how to love themselves, they will automatically know how it feels and the feelings that can be created by someone else that naturally loves them. When we learn how to love ourselves, our homes will be happier. When we learn how to love ourselves, our marriages will flourish. When we learn how to love ourselves, we are happier because of the difference we're making in our lives and another person's life. Loving yourself is okay! As a matter of fact, it's required of you. But on the contrary, be careful not to go overboard with loving yourself to the degree you can't love anyone else because you are in love with yourself. This kind of love is a selfish and proud love. This love does not reflect what Mark 12:31 is referring to when it comes to love.

Throughout this book, I want to encourage couples that are serious about making their relationships work to talk to one another about:

- How do you give love? (What do they do for you to show their love to you?)

- How do you receive love? (What makes them feel or believe you love them?)

By doing this, you will let each other know how you expect to be loved.

It is my desire for you to read this book and begin to develop the wisdom that comes from understanding Mark 12:31, and other verses throughout this book with the understanding. It's important for us to get this because it is possible to be in love with someone and not know **how** to love them, or to love being around someone and not know how to take **care** of them while you're with them.

Open Ses·a·me has the potential to open your eyes, ears, and your heart if you allow yourself to be open. Many people don't think about verses such as, "Thou shalt Love thy Neighbor as thyself" seriously in the relationship arena. Have you? Can you truly say, "Yes, I love myself?" And I know how to translate that love to others? Unfortunately, not everyone can say this. There are people in relationships who don't know how to take care or love themselves, as a result, they can't take care of or love others. It's hard for them to do this, especially in the time we are living in where everything seems to promote "selfie-ness", or selfishness and self-centeredness. I'm not saying that there's no hope; I'm just saying there lies one of the reasons why I wrote this book.

As you continue to read this book, try to stop, think, and relate to some of the stories and see how things in your life can be changed with simple suggestions. I pray that you enjoy my book, Open Ses·a·me. Now, let's start unlocking hidden doors.

Remember your mate is the closest neighbor you will ever have.

Calling You to Fix-It

He sent them to the Lord to ask, "Are you the one who was to come, or should we expect someone else?" Luke 7:19 (NIV)

"Are you the **ONE**? Or should I expect **SOMEONE else?**"

Have you ever asked your spouse, girlfriend or boyfriend this question while thinking to yourself "You can't be the **one**? Because the **one** that is for me should be making me happy!

While sitting in prison awaiting death, John sent his disciples to ask **Jesus** if He was the ONE. John wanted to know if He was the ONE to come to save all humanity, and I would go as far as saying John *needed* to hear that Jesus was the ONE. They all believed He was, but I believe they asked Him to see if they could prompt Jesus into action because of what John was facing in his life.

Isn't it strange how people (including myself) can become so blind to what we know to be true, but due to our current circumstances we depend on other people to come to our rescue?

What happened with those disciples can easily happen in any relationship. Someone can be in a financial bind, behind in their work, hungry, or all in their feelings because of lustful desires, and still expect the person closest to them to know automatically what's wrong and how to "Fix-It."

I believe the reason John was hesitant or asking if Jesus was the One was because of what he was going through personally. John was in a hard position for doing the will of God. John was sitting in prison with death in his future. He wanted someone to fix his situation. That's why he asked Jesus this question. He knew Jesus was the One; he knew Jesus was the Messiah. And yet, he became blind; and couldn't see because of what he was going through. Jesus experienced the same thing when he was fa-ced with the cross in Luke 22:42:

Saying, Father, if thou be willing, remove this cup from me: nevertheless not my will, but thine, be done.

Let's keep in mind that relationships are never one-sided. One gives a little, and the other gives a little. What happened between John and Jesus may happen in our relationships, especially for those who are married, when one person is looking to the other for help in hard times, and in those times, no help is found.

What I want to unlock here are the thoughts and expectations that can be developed in relationships when someone believes their mate is supposed to make them happy all the time. Could it be that the one being looked to for help can't help with that particular problem?

There will be times when the only person that can help us with us is God. No matter how bad we want our spouse, boyfriend/girlfriend to get us out of the problem, we have to walk through it with Him.

Being in a relationship with someone is in itself hard because you are dealing with two individuals with different make-ups and different personalities. There will be times where it can be hard to figure out the difference between God helping you feel better, and your mate making you feel better.

There were times early in our marriage when I would be stressed out from work or down-and-out over not being able to visit my family and friends as much as I used to; whereas, in the past I could visit them as often as I wanted. Because I was growing up and had a family and had started taking on the responsibilities of a man, I couldn't see or talk to them as much as I would have liked.

> **Therefore shall a man leave his father and his mother, and shall cleave unto his wife: and they shall be one flesh.**
> **Genesis 2:24**

In those moments of feeling homesick and needing to get out and interact with my family, I would look to Robyn to give me what I needed. But I began to notice that even though Robyn and I were going on dates and talking, there was still something in me that wasn't satisfied. I needed something else, but nothing we did helped or provided what I needed. I had to learn that God was the answer, and not Robyn. I wanted and expected Robyn to fix my problems because she was right there. When she didn't, I blamed her for my lack of fulfillment and shamefully thought to myself that I must need another.

I can remember telling Robyn that no one goes to the doctor with a broken arm and expects the doctor to say, "Well what do you want me to do about it?" Or "I don't know how to fix your problem." I would ask Robyn, "Do you see what I'm saying? I need you to fix me," because I expected her to fix me. I looked at her, and she looked at me. I thought to myself, "*I must have married the wrong woman.*" She talked to God and said, "That's not my job!!!" I didn't understand that Robyn couldn't be my doctor. I had unrealistic expectations for my wife. I didn't realize that only God could fix me.

Soothed or Cured
Medicines such as Aspirin and Tylenol are to be taken to relieve pain and fever for up to 4 to 8 hours. However, they don't cure you of your discomfort; they only relieve you long enough for your body to try to fix itself from whatever is wrong with you. If one isn't careful, they will begin to believe that just because they've stopped feeling the pain, the medicine cured them. But those who have an understanding of how medicine works know that the medicine only soothes and relieves the body from the pain temporarily.

Through immaturity and ignorance, people believe in things that aren't real. Because it either looks or feels real, it's hard for those people to tell the difference.

Before marrying Robyn, I was expecting her to be everything I needed. (Robyn most likely had the same expectations of me, too.) I expected that when I was hungry, she would feed me. When I was tired, she would say something that could wake me up. Whatever question I had, she should have the answer.

I carried this mindset for a long time in the beginning of our marriage, hoping and praying for her to change. I wanted to believe that Robyn could cure all my hurts.

Robyn could soothe me, but she couldn't cure me. She could do things around the house for me. She could keep the kids quiet while I rested, but she couldn't cure me to the extent that I had no problems or worries. It wasn't her place or responsibility. She was just there to help support me until I got through whatever it was I was going through.

There were times when she managed things so well that it almost seemed like she had done everything for me, but I couldn't fully depend on her to do everything for me. I would tell my good friend, Marques, that if our mates were perfect, then we wouldn't need Jesus. If I were to come home to my favorite meal waiting for me, Robyn wearing my favorite outfit (her birthday suit) with a cup of lemonade Kool-Aid in her hand, and the TV turned to ESPN for me every day, ☺ I would be like Jesus who? Just kidding! Robyn's dreams were for me to take her to the Mall and buy whatever purse or purses she wanted, while finding the perfect shoes to match, just spending the whole day walking and talking with her man. ☺ We all have our dreams, but back to the story…

We have to understand that we must run our individual Race because we have our own purpose to fulfill. We should thank God for giving us someone to share our lives with, but we cannot get it confused. We must look to the only ONE that can heal us, and take care of the one that can soothe us. It's not their responsibility, and it's not fair to them. We must seek God first, and everything else will be added unto us.

> **But seek ye first the kingdom of God,
> and his righteousness; and all these things
> shall be added unto you.
> Matthew 6:33 KJV**

The way to unlock this door is to understand that your mate is not supposed to heal you but to soothe you from the pains of life. God is the doctor. Your mate is there to comfort you while the doctor is working on you.

Love That Comes First

Jesus answered them and said, Verily, verily, I say unto you, Ye seek me, not because ye saw the miracles, but because ye did eat of the loaves, and were filled. John 6:26 KJV

In this passage, we hear Jesus accusing some of those who are following Him of just coming along because of the benefits that come from being in His presence. He explains to them that they're not paying any attention to the miracles as evidence that He is the Son of God. All they cared about were the earthly things. They cared about those things that are meaningless and will disappear over time.

Have you ever been in a relationship and thought to yourself, *this person is only with me because I _____.*

Well, my wife and I have. In the early years of our marriage, we both had those exact thoughts. I thought to myself, *"She's only with me because I go to work, go to church, and take care of her and the kids."* She thought to herself, *"He's only with me because of the kids."* We looked at each other through **immature** eyes; eyes of assumption; eyes that were unfamiliar and unaware of the truth that was right there in front of them. We just assumed everything was good. We weren't aware of the details of each other's lives.

Immaturity can be defined by not being brought to a complete state. One still in the process of development.

Locked behind a hidden door of suspicion, Robyn and I would tell each other jokes like, "You don't really love me." Or, "You don't really care anything about me. All you really care about is making sure everything is o.k."

One of the things Robyn and I had to learn early on in our marriage (especially when we were both working our 9 to 5's), was that the reason we didn't talk about how our day went was because we were both trying to forget what had happened earlier that day, either at home or work. We thought that if we didn't talk about it, we wouldn't have to re-live it, especially if it was something that got on our nerves or rubbed us the wrong way. Say for instance, if some guy flirted with Robyn on the job or if a boss offended me, we preferred not to talk about that particular incident. We didn't want to get worked up after calming down, or we didn't want the other to get worked up over nothing.

But for us to get to the place where we could see and love each other for who we were, we had to grow together and mature into people that could see. I had to mature into the man who could love the woman he married, and not treat her like his babies' momma. She had to grow into the woman who could love the man she married and not just the fun guy that pays the bills, plays with the kids and takes her out on Friday nights. We had to learn to love the person and not their resume. We had to love each other for who we were, and not just for what we were bringing to the table.

The Resume
The "Resume" is a person's past mixed with their present that qualifies them as a good candidate to date or marry in the future. It's a good idea to have a person with potential, achievements, and goals in life. We just can't make that our main focus.

For almost any athlete, business person, or anyone doing something of significance, the first thing we notice is their talent and how well they perform. Then, we look at all of their possessions, and then we look at the person. The greater their role, the higher they will go, the more they will have, and more reasons why someone should be with them.

We see only the exterior, their resume. When being with someone of significance or insignificance, we must look passed all of his or her accomplishments and failures to see them for who they really are.

When it comes to knowing Jesus, we have to understand that just knowing *of* Him & *of* His benefits is not enough. Our intent should not just be to linger along with the crowd following Jesus to gather the "crumbs" of His benefits. Our intent should be to take hold of the benefits that come with believing, trusting, and following Christ. That should be our main focal point. We should keep Jesus first and put everything else behind Him.

Make Him First

Luke 7:37-38 NKJV says, "There was a woman in the city who was a sinner, when she knew that *Jesus* sat at the table in the Pharisee's house, she brought an alabaster flask of fragrant oil, [38] and stood at His feet behind *Him* weeping; and she began to wash His feet with her tears, and wiped *them* with the hair of her head; and she kissed His feet and anointed *them* with the fragrant oil."

When I read these verses, I see a story of a person that loves Jesus for who He is. If you paid attention, Jesus hadn't done anything for her yet. She took it upon herself to go to him and worship Him. She got word that Jesus was near, and went. Jesus didn't have to do anything for her to go to Him, wash His feet, and kiss them. Nor did He have to tell her to do so. To put it simply, this woman loved Jesus and worshipped Him for who He was to her.

At the beginning of our marriage, Robyn and I failed at this. We loved each other for the wrong reasons because we had our priorities out of order. When we first started "going together," all we would talk about was where we wanted to work, what we wanted to do in church, and how many kids we wanted. Back then we had really intimate and personal conversations about our future together. In the boyfriend/girlfriend stage of our relationship we had our priorities in line, but once we got married, things changed.

We took on more responsibilities with work, church, and with our kids. We completely overlooked the person that was performing the duties (Robyn and me). All we talked about was how we hated work, enjoyed church, and all the new stuff the kids were doing. It was good that we were keeping each other up to date on everything. The bad thing was that we weren't talking about God or ourselves.

We got our priorities wrong by taking our eyes off of each other. We got tired and stopped caring for one another. We lost our first love and interest. When we did this, we started looking at each other through immature eyes and hard eyes.

Remember love between each other should always come first; not work, kids, sports, or church. Love is the thing that brought you two together in the first place.

Unlock each other from your responsibilities and keep your priorities in order early on in your relationship.

Love
Love is a living thing.
Love is an endless thing.
Love should be meaningful.
Love can be earned.
Love should be shared.
Love should be told.
Love can't be bought nor can love be sold.
When allowed your love can grow.
When allowed your love can die.
The option is yours and mine just how far love can go.
Love

Love Me for Me

One day in my time of prayer, God led me to study 1 Corinthians 13. It was there that I began to understand what true love is and how I was to practice it on Robyn. He made me realize that I had been doing wrong, and showed me how He dealt with me in the past when I was doing wrong. When He was showing me "me", this question came up: Who was I to demand more from Robyn when she missed the mark when I was missing the mark worse than she was?

I went to Robyn and told her about biblical love, and suggested that we both should begin to demonstrate what godly love is. The Bible says in 1 Corinthians 13:4-7 in the NLT that:

> [4] Love is patient and kind. Love is not jealous or boastful or proud [5] or rude. It does not demand its own way. It is not irritable, and it keeps no record of being wronged. [6] It does not rejoice about injustice but rejoices whenever the truth wins out. [7] Love never gives up, never loses faith, is always hopeful, and endures through every circumstance.

Verse 8 begins with: **"Love never fails"**. We recognized that we had been failing the whole time. We had lost sight of what defined true love. We were no longer patient and kind to each other.

I had completely forgotten and stopped caring that I was the one that said, "*Yes,* I will take this woman to be my wedded wife. I will take her to live together after God's ordinance in Holy Matrimony, and to have and to hold through sickness and health. To comfort her, honor her, and love her while forsaking ALL others. To keep myself only unto her as long as we both should live."

Robyn and I made a covenant not to give up on each other nor lose faith in our marriage. We agreed always to be hopeful and to endure through all the better or worse moments we vowed before God and ourselves.

But what do you do when you find a hidden door to love in your relationship? The key is to:

- Recognize your faults.
- Purpose in your heart to face issues and problems so that you both can talk through them.
- Turn loose any old grudges that you may have kept hidden away.

I believe Paul wrote those verses as the foundational principles of love. Will it be easy? Of course Not …Will you fix-it over night? No! Will it be fun and exciting? Sometimes! Is your relationship worth it? Yes.

Unlocking *You to Love Me*

Here we are!

Robyn and I have always expressed to one another how we both wanted someone to love us for who we really are. Here's our layout of what we believe makes us who we are.

Ben is:	Robyn is:
God's Boy "Jr"	The Wife
The Husband	The Mother
The Father	The Teacher
The Friend/Brother	The Friend/Sister
+ The Worker	+ The Person Everyone Knows
= Ben the Person	= God's Girl

For me, there's Ben, the man that no one knows exists. I call him "JR". Then there's Ben the guy who doesn't have it all together, even though he appears to. And then, there is Ben who is trying to learn as much as he can about how to raise four daughters, so that he won't break his daughters. The one who can't tell you everything that he and his guy friends are talking about, and Ben the man who has to work overtime because the job requires it even though he would rather be home with his family. Then there's Ben the man who knows his wife and family deserve more, but he doesn't know how to give it to them; the man that believes: *The true soldier fights not because he hates what's in front of him, but because he loves what's behind him.* – G.K. Chesterton.

Robyn, she is the woman that will follow her man anywhere. She is the woman that conceived, delivered, and nurtured five kids. Most people call her Mrs. Freeman. She is a wonderful listener and has a smile that can calm those around her without even speaking to them. And then there is Robyn the *lil' girl* everyone knows her to be, but God knows her as someone else and greater even if she doesn't see it in herself.

Robyn and I would go back and forth with each other with different scenarios about how we are expected to treat each other. I told her that one of the reasons I didn't want to be with someone that would only love me for my resume was because of the fear that if I stopped being the thing she wanted, she might not continue to love me for me. If I lost my job and had nothing to give, would she still love me? If I had a nervous breakdown, would she stay with me? If God placed it on my heart and I believed that we should move to Texas away from her family, without a plan and holding onto only a belief – would she follow me? I wanted to know if she would and could be faithful to our vows in the better or worse moments.

Hidden in my heart was fear. I was afraid of the answer. During tough conversations, I could hear Robyn agreeing in word, but I could see the doubt on her face.

I saw it when she talked about being Robyn the *Mother* or Robyn the *Friend* because being Robyn the Friend and Robyn the mother is easier than being Robyn the *Wife*, who had a hard time keeping up with Ben the Husband. I noticed her having thoughts such as, "*I wonder if he would stay if I choose to be Robyn the Mother over being Robyn the Wife? I wonder if Ben the Friend can be faithful to Robyn the Wife?*"

We both had questions early on that were hidden within ourselves that needed to be unlocked. Just like someone fumbling through a key ring to unlock a door in a hurry, Robyn and

I were fumbling our way through our marriage.

    I would recommend that you and your mate sit down and fill out this graph and recite the confession at the end. Go over your responsibilities and personalities to find out what roles are easier for each of you. Robyn and I have unlocked many doors to each other by being able to see each other for who we really are and who we would rather be. You may be amazed at how often you are someone else and not who you think you are. You may find that your mate sees you as someone else. You may even find that your mate is one person, but would rather be someone else.

    We all have different responsibilities, personalities, and hats that we must put on from time to time. We have to learn how to love each role that our mate has to be if we want to love them for who they truly are.

We must recognize that it will come only through a constant and vital application that will take a lifetime to perfect. Be encouraged to go over your vows with your mate and by yourself. Take it one verse at a time, let the Spirit of God help you, and love you where you are.

The opportunity is there and the option is yours.

Your name here_____	Your mates name here_____
The _____	The _____
The _____	The _____
The _____	The _____
The _____	The _____
+The _____	+The _____
= God's_____	= God's_____

Answer these questions:

Who are you?
1. _____ _____

Who do most people know you as?
2. _____ _____

How many roles do you think you have?
3. _____ _____

Who do you know your mate as?
4. _____ _____

How many roles do you think your mate has?
5. _____ _____

Which ones of yourself do you love more?
6. _____ _____

Which ones do you love less?
7. _____   _____

Recite this about yourself:

<u>I AM</u> patient and kind. <u>I AM</u> not jealous or boastful or proud or rude. <u>I</u> do not demand my own way. <u>I</u> am not irritable, and <u>I</u> keep no record of being wronged. <u>I</u> do not rejoice about injustice but rejoices whenever the truth wins out. <u>I</u> never gives up, <u>I</u> never lose faith, <u>I AM</u> always hopeful, and <u>I</u> endures through every circumstance. -I am Love.

The Bottle

Once upon a time, there was a certain man that was a recovering alcoholic. He had been clean for the past eight months, and for the first time, was looking forward to being able to say that he has been sober for 12 months.

He lived an average life with his wife and kids, working the day shift at a manufacturing facility. One day after work, one of his friends came over to him as he was walking to his truck asked him, "Have you heard? They plan on laying off 50 to 100 employees by the end of September."

This certain man had been working there for the past three years and was in the running for a promotion. A lay-off was the furthest thing from his mind. He was just starting to get the pep back in his step. His wife was just starting to get her glow back because he was really recovering and their marriage had hope again.

So the certain man sat in his truck and dropped his keys in his lap and thought to himself, *Not Now, This can't happen now. I'm just getting started.* The thought *Go get a beer* flew across his mind, "No, No! No!" he said, aloud, to himself, "I'm not going back to being that man again. I'm going to be a good boy," he said jokingly.

Picking up his keys, he turned on his truck and started home. His phone buzzed with a new text message from Billy Boy. *Have you heard? Meet us at the corner store so we can talk about this.*" Knowing what Billy Boy meant, the certain man texted back; *I'll have to meet you another time. I'm headed home.* "Not today!" he said jokingly, trying to motivate himself so he could get it off his mind. When he'd made it home, he was welcomed with "Heys" and "Hugs" by his family.

A few days later, his wife asked if he could stop on his way home and get some milk and tissue. "No problem babe, I can do that," he replied. Getting to the store, the first thing he saw was a big **On Sale** sign. **24 pack for only $15.99. Get it while it's cold.** Smiling, he walked past the sign, but he ran into another sale sign, **Only $12.99 for an 18 pack.** By this time, he could feel that, what use to be, dead feeling coming back alive in the middle of his belly, right beneath his chest. It was like something was growing in his body. He reminded himself, "You're only in here for milk and plastic wrap." *What?* "No, I'm in here for milk and tissue." Right, he said, "Milk and tissue what was I thinking."

Grabbing the milk, he walked by another sign but this time there were single beer cans in an ice chest for anyone to just grab and go. **"$1.29 ea."** He thought to himself, "*When did they start putting it in the middle of the aisles like this? They should make this place an ABC store with all this alcohol in here.*"

As he was in the checkout line, that certain man's cell rang, it was his wife. She asked, "Hey babe, will you pick up some plastic wrap when you get the milk and tissue." "What?" he replied, "I mean yeah, yeah I can get it. Is there anything else you can think of before I leave? "No that's it." She said, "Thanks, babe. Hey, I'm so glad you're doing better and not struggling anymore. It means a lot to me. But I'm not going to keep you. I know you're busy. We'll talk when you get home. I love you."

With the jug of milk in one hand and a pack of tissue in the other he walked back by the ice chest and grabbed one. "No, No, No!" he said to himself, placing it back into the ice. He went straight to the plastic wrap. "Got it," he said. "Now I'm out of here."

Walking out the store, he could feel his insides pulling him. Struggling with the temptation to go back and get a drink. He began breathing fast, his heart began racing, his arms begin feeling as light as balloons floating off his body. "No," he said to himself, "I can't, and I won't."

Jumping into his truck, he pulled off. The Low Fuel light came on as he was driving down the road. "Dog!" he said. Turning into the gas station he had another thought. *Remember this place? It has the best deals around.* He said, "No, I'm just here for gas." Slipping in his debit card, he got $20 in gas and left. "Good job," he said to himself in a quiet voice. *You fool*, shouted a loud voice in his head, *"You're missing out on everything. You think you can handle this on your own? Your Job, Your wife, your kids, and the money! You are crazy! You need a drink to help you think. One won't hurt! You done turned into a pushover, a Kool-Aid drinking, a one- woman having Do Boy!"*

"Get ye behind me Satan," the man blurted out as he

pulled into his driveway. "Daddy! You got the milk, and the tissue too. Now I can wipe my behind," his son said as they walked together into the house. With a big hug and thank you from his wife, he settled in at home.

Later that night his wife asked him, "Baby can you go get me some gas? I forgot to on the way home, and I know I'm not going to want to get it in the morning." He replied, "Yeah babe. I can do that." Forgetting what had happened earlier, he threw on some pants, grabbed his license and some cash, and headed out the door to the gas station.

On the way, he heard that loud voice again, "*Yes! We can still get a bottle!*" He could feel his body coming alive. He started breathing stronger, and he was losing control of his body. The Old Man was back. It was like something pushed him aside telling him exactly what to do and where to go. He walked straight to the back of the store and got his favorite drink. He laid his license, the cash, and the bottle down. The cashier said, "I haven't seen you in a while. Are you sure you want that?" "Yeah!" he said in an aggravated tone. *"No,"* he said in a low, quiet voice in his head. "What am I doing," he asked himself, "I came here for gas, not beer." It was like he was watching himself commit this act through the security camera.

After pumping the gas, he left. Looking to his right, he saw the bottle sitting there waiting to be opened. Fussing with himself on what to do, he said, "I need to stop and pour this out." "*You can't,*" the voice quickly said. "*If you get pulled over you'll be charged with having an open container. Just keep it and get rid of it when you get home.*" "Dog-gone-it," he said to himself, "I thought I was over this, and look – here I go again. I'm not going to drink it." "*Sure you won't,*" he heard the voice say.

"I'm not," he said with an aggravated voice.

Making it home and hoping his wife would be up so he could tell her what was happening, he found her asleep. Grabbing the bottle because he couldn't leave it in her car, he set it on the table. Pacing around the kitchen, he said, "I got to come up with a plan to get rid of this, but what do I do?" Sitting at the table, he was now having a staring match with the bottle, thinking to himself, "*What is going on with me? Do I? Or don't I? Should I? Or shouldn't I? What if? Or if not?*"

It was like his body had a mind of its own. He was no longer in control. Grabbing the bottle he popped the top and put it to his mouth. When the taste hit his lips, he said, "NO. I am not that man anymore." He stood up, poured the beer out and said, "Enough is enough." Throwing the bottle in the trash, he went and got in the shower, singing and praising God for giving him the strength to carry on and not fall into temptation. He jumped in the bed, holding onto to his wife, he fell asleep.

Morning came, and his wife found the receipt. She found the bottle and her stomach dropped. Her heart stopped, and she froze up. "*Not now and not again!*" she cried out on the inside and fell to the floor weeping. The certain man walked in, still singing and praising and ready for a new day. He looked at his beautiful wife and asked, "Baby, what's wrong?" She looked up and said, "How could you? It's been eight months and why now? What happened? Why couldn't you? Why did you?"

Have you ever experienced this? Were you the man or the woman? Have you ever received a text, e-mail, or even a missed call from a wrong number that set you and your mate back even though nothing happened? Here lies what once was an open door in a growing and recovering relationship that has now became a shut and hidden door to someone's life, due to a bump in a relationship. Have you ever experienced a moment when your present looks a lot like your past? These moments can feel like a sucker punch to the gut or a slap in the face. It's a sensitive space that has to stay open to heal.

Proceed

Who's right? Who's wrong?

The evidence is there.

The experience is there.

The proof is there.

Her hands held the evidence and her heart has the experience.

Did she have every right to cuss and fuss and cry? Yes.

The man on the other hand couldn't believe what was going

on. He woke up on top of the world but is being seen as low as dirt.

So what does one do when all is well between them and the Lord, but not so well between them and everyone else? What does one do when their word doesn't mean a hill-of-beans anymore? What can someone do when all the evidence is against him or her? What does one do when they know things could have been a lot worse if they had proceeded, but they did the right thing? What does one do when they can say, *"Yes I was at the door, but I didn't go in?"* The old me was there, but the new me showed up. I am guilty to an extent, but I am not guilty to that degree.

My answer to them is to believe what the Lord says:

Even if we feel guilty, God is greater than our feelings, and he knows everything. 1 John 3:20 (NLT)

Continue to live your life until your words begin to mean something again. Don't lock un-forgiveness in your heart, but understand where others are coming from. Things were beginning to become better for them. They were beginning to be happy again. They were beginning to trust you and see you as the person they knew you could be. A test came, and you passed, but it looked like you failed to them. Live your life and try your best to move forward, not having to have to prove yourself. If you're like the wife in this story, try to believe and trust in him again. Don't assume the facts. Your feelings and thoughts are understandable because of your experience. Try to pray for a better understanding of what happened. You can't forget the past hurt and pain, but through God's grace, you can move forward and don't focus on them, or re-live them. It's a reason why it's called the past.

    I want to recommend that you look this over with your mate, talk about it, and don't fight over it. Just talk. It's important that you do because it's easy to jump to conclusions when you have had a bad experience in a relationship. Yes, you and I know what happened in this story, but it's easy to forget when it's happening to you. Don't allow an open area in your life to become a closed and hidden exit in your relationship due to someone jumping to conclusions. Protect that area of your life because trust is kept in that room.

Trust Takes Years to Build. Seconds to Break. And Forever to Repair

Unlock the cap to The Bottle.

Unlocking   *Comparison*

Comparison

Not too many couples have conversations about the topic of *Comparison,* but we all expect our mate to know not to do it and why. In this chapter we will be going over some dos, don'ts, and why not's when it comes to comparing your mate to others. Let me warn you that when you see a <u>Blank</u> use your imagination to figure out what I mean. I will begin like always with ladies first, and then with my wife's help, gentlemen.

Ladies: There is no comparison when it comes to your man. Your man is the only man like himself, and that's the way he wants to keep it. So when you compare your man to another man, it's like saying to your man, I think his <u>Blank</u> is bigger than yours. You may just be talking about his hair or his shoes or even his car or job, but all your man hears when you compare him to another man is, I think he has a big <u>Blank</u> and it's better than yours.

That's it! That's all he's hearing, and that's how he's taking it. So when you say things like, "Hey babe, I want you to wear your clothes like him!" Or, "I wonder how he keeps it all together like he does?" Or, "I think you should cut your hair like his." Or, "He always does things with his wife and kids." Or, "Why won't you buy me a house or car like theirs. Or, I wish we could do stuff like them." Or "Do you think he struggles with __Blank__ like you do?"

Pretty much anything that involves another man or anything that he is doing should not be compared in any way at all around your man. Why you might ask. Because it's like you saying: I think he has a big __Blank__ and I bet his is better than yours. That's how he is hears it.

Have you ever made a comment to your husband, boyfriend, or just some dude you know, and for some odd reason they gave you a reaction that just made you say, "My bad, I didn't mean for you to take it so seriously." Or have any of them ever said, "If you like him so much you should just go be with him then." I bet you have and I bet you didn't know why he reacted the way he did. I'll tell you why. Because you just crossed the line of the unknown by saying I think his __Blank__ is bigger than yours.

My wife would say things like that, and it would just make me angrier than a little boy who just got turned away at a lemonade stand after waiting ten minutes to get his favorite drink. Fortunately, we got over this after we talked about it.

Freeze- Activity Time: Ask your man about a bad question or statement that you've asked him. Be prepared for the truth, and stop comparing him to other men.

Gentlemen: Women are very delicate creatures. They either love who they are or struggle with loving who they are. When you compare your wife, woman, or girlfriend to another, she

Unlocking   *Comparison*

will react in one of three ways. First, she's going to fuss at you and question you for desiring the woman you're comparing her to. Second, cry because she's already insecure about the thing you're comparing her about, or bottle up how she feels by saying absolutely NOTHING. But don't worry. Whatever she bottles up will eventually EXPLODE out of her like a shaken up bottle of soda. (If you've never seen this from a woman, it's BAD, really BAD; like a rocket into space BAD). The final thing that a woman may do is to try to turn into the person you're comparing her to for fear that you will leave her for someone else. When a man really loves his woman (and his health), he should NEVER compare her to another woman (as long as they both shall live). Just make suggestions WITHOUT attaching any woman's name to that suggestion. For example, Ben would say, "Man, Mrs. Such in Such looked good in those jeans ☹ Or Man Ole girl has a good hair-do☹." Everybody say bad move Ben, Rookie Mistake man.

Men, don't be like This Ben, Love the woman you have enough to help her "enhance" what she has and not "transform" her into someone else. Remember she's God's daughter and your Woman of God.

Unlocking Comparison

As two authentic people in a relationship, Robyn and I had to stop comparing ourselves to other people. It was causing such division between the two of us that we both felt that neither of us had any room for error when it came to just sitting down to express our thoughts or feelings toward each other. So what we came up with was to just ***stop.*** We began to pay close attention to the signs that were all around us so that we could avoid the potholes of criticism that would turn into rejection from fallen rocks of hard words. We had to avoid conflicts by saying things like, "I think that would look good on you" or "I think that may be fun to try, what do you think?"

It may seem like this is playing a role or pretending, but REALLY it's you learning how to talk to one another in a respectful way. At least until you're both able to speak to one another in a respectful way without even trying. Keep in mind that we're all humans and we will make mistakes, so we all have to try our best not to screw things up with our mates. It may not seem like much to some, but others will appreciate it.

Comparing causes conflict. Complimenting causes companionship.

Couples

The problems and issues we often face in our relationships are there because we just weren't taught about them. In the book of Titus, we find helpful information that offers sound guidance. This guidance not only changes us but also shapes us to be individuals of integrity. We are shaped to be role models and teachers to others, who for whatever reason just haven't learned the things Titus taught. In the following verse, you will see that Titus is speaking to men.

> ⁶ Likewise exhort the young men to be sober-minded, ⁷ in all things showing yourself to be a pattern of good works; in doctrine showing integrity, reverence, incorruptibility, ⁸ sound speech that cannot be condemned, that one who is an opponent may be ashamed, having nothing evil to say of you.
> **Titus 2:6-8 (NKJV)**

In this next verse, you will see Titus speaking to women.

> ³ the older women likewise, that they

> be reverent in behavior, not slanderers, not given to much wine, teachers of good things-- ⁴ that they admonish the young women to love their husbands, to love their children, ⁵ to be discreet, chaste, homemakers, good, obedient to their own husbands, that the word of God may not be blasphemed. **Titus 2:3-5 (NKJV)**

Titus has given us principles for a strong and healthy marriage. In times past, such principles as Titus presents here were taught as a matter of tradition. They were taught in the church or passed from mother to daughter, father to son. These principles were part of the daily lives of adult role models who lived by them. For some reason, many young men and women today aren't being taught these principles, resulting in a huge problem in marriage, and society as a whole.

My wife and I had to learn how to talk about personal experiences and different mindsets because these are the things that unlocked hidden doors in our relationships. When communicating as adults, and not as children who point fingers and call each other names, we were able to overcome open jealousy and hidden fears. We had to take it upon ourselves to read and study the Bible to face *True Truth* and not what we thought to be true to us because things are different now that we are married as opposed to when we were single.

Single Men

Some men may say that it's hard to find a good woman when there are so many different types of single women looking for a single man to marry. It's hard for him to keep himself to himself when so many women are willing to do whatever it takes to get him. Most women don't understand that a man doesn't want a woman that does everything other women are doing. A man wants a woman that stands out; a woman that doesn't always go with the flow of the world. Is it entertaining to see fifteen (+) women competing for one man? *Yes.* But does it make sense? *No.* What it is though is foolish. I'm not calling them fools. I'm just saying that what they're doing is foolish. A woman is worth much more than that, and she can do and be better than that

Single Women

From talking to my wife and my sister, I know that it can be hard for a woman to keep herself pure for God when there are many different voices and expectations out there, especially if she wasn't taught the importance and purpose of keeping herself pure. It's important that women understand that a man will do whatever you let him do. I'm going to tell you like I told my sister Alicia, *"To be a wonderful wife, you have to first be a terrible girlfriend."* This means you have to keep your goods to yourself. He will be mad, but a real man will respect you even more if you do. I know you may struggle with the desire for love and affection. But if you can hold out and show him that you live to a higher standard and that you are willing to follow him as long as he lives to a higher standard, you will weed out a lot of "Jo Blows" and a lot of headaches. And, you will both be that much closer to a better relationship. *A "Jo Blow" is a guy you wouldn't want your daughter, mother, sister, auntie, female friends or cousins dating.*

There are so many different types of men and women with so many different needs and wants. It's hard for one person to believe that they can be everything and give everything to one person without their mate looking to another for what they're

Unlocking *Couples*

lacking. In this day and age, all you have to do is look at your phone or social media and there it is, avenues to people and information.

I would like to go over scenarios that are common for most people, but for some reason still hidden behind doors. We can continue to get ourselves into tough situations with the opposite sex by making these mistakes. Let's look at the following groups of people. You have:

The Business Man   The Working Man   The Praying Man

The Praying Woman   The Working Woman   The Mommy

Unlocking Couples

Unlocking   *Couples*

Do you know how easy it is for a man or woman to fall for someone with different morals or marital status, or just because they work together, or go to school or church together, or anything like that?   Use the people from the previous page. You can have a married man having a hard time managing everything, and a single woman can walk up to him and offer to help him and in that one moment, his whole day can change. Or with a married woman, a single man could come up to her and tell her how beautiful she is today and make her whole day brighter.

You could have a single woman who goes to church, goes to work, has studied all the *How to Be a Good Wife* books, and has a bright future ahead of her, but she just keeps running into "*Jo Blows*" that only want her for her body and her independence. They only want her because she can take care of herself and them, and he doesn't have to do anything for her. She's a single woman who believes that better is out there, and she is just waiting to **be** the wife she believes she **is** and is **ready** to do everything she has learned to do (with her ready to be married self).

So this single woman runs into a man who is married. He is tired, hurt, scared, quiet (because he doesn't believe that he has anyone he can talk to that can understand him) and he's in the mood for loving. But he  keeps on going because he understands his responsibility and his hope for a better future to come.

Imagine what happens when these two people's paths

cross, it's like life has **exploded** back into their lives but they are off limits to one another. The married man looks at her and sees his old wife, the woman she used to be. The single woman looks to the married man and sees the type of husband she always wanted. They both have thoughts like:

 What do we do?
How can we continue?
Is this really wrong?

They both believe: "I can be and do everything to you that you need!"

These are tough questions and tough situations that my wife and I had to face for us to protect our marriage. My wife is a beautiful woman. Any man would love to have a chance with her. There were times when I was so busy that I overlooked her and didn't pay her the attention she needed, and some joker would tell her the things that I should have been saying to make her feel appreciated and worthy and pretty. On the other hand, there have been times when I needed her to talk to me and look at me as a man of worth, mainly in the times when I didn't feel worthy or when I didn't know what decision to make for my family. I had to sit down with my wife and tell her that there are three things that I need from her. They are:

1. Her Scent.
2. Her Touch.
3. Her Voice.

I need these three things in our relationship. Her needs are:

1. For me to let her know that I'm not leaving.
2. For me to compliment her beauty.
3. For me to do and be all that God demands of me to be.

List 3 things you and your mate believe you need in your relationship with each other.

1. _____   _____

2. _____   _____

3. _____   _____

These six things unlocked our hidden fears in our marriage that opened our relationship to see the true worth of each other, placing a higher value on our marriage. We had to take it upon ourselves to learn this because those six things aren't spelled out in the Bible. Robyn and I had to teach each other not to judge one another for being human. We both made rookie mistakes early on in our marriage, and from time to time we still do. Fortunately, we handle one another a lot better than we use to. We had to learn from each other to help one another, so we could protect our relationship from the distractions that were all around us. As a couple that wanted to stay together, we owed it to ourselves to be safe in this crazy relationship filled world.

Need or Greed

There are certain essentials that human beings need, things such as food, water, shelter, and companionship. There are also things that are such a benefit to us we believe that we need them, things such as television, smart phones, and top of the line clothes. I believe we all can agree that those are some much needed items that make life easier.

Now, what I would like to go over in this chapter are two interesting but touchy topics that have to be unlocked for your relationship to flourish and be protected from hidden desires, hidden intentions, hidden deceptions, or hidden expectations.

Many times in broken relationships the question comes up, *why did or why do you feel that you needed to do that?* Or *why do you feel and believe so strongly that you need that?* Because in the back of the person's mind they're thinking, "*I would have done that for you!* Or *you didn't have to go out and get something new; I had it.*"

Many people that have been cheated on or done wrong and left alone still have that unanswered question. As we read on, let's lighten the mood and look over some scenarios and some reasons.

I'm sure you have heard the saying Men are all Dogs, and they only want one thing. This saying isn't true for everyone, but unfortunately, there are those who have made a bad name for themselves.

'Why must I be like that? Why must I chase the cat?" some men may ask themselves. In my opinion, the world has taught us as men to believe that it's nothing but the dog in us that makes us chase the cat. If you ask any man that has matured about why he ran so many women, he'll tell you that he didn't know any better, and if he did he wouldn't have treated his ex-lovers so badly. I've spoken with many men, and most of them have told me that they weren't thinking about seeing her as a sister in Christ. All they cared about was their need and how it was about to be met.

Take me for instance. As a man, I believe I need sex. I believe I need to make love to my wife. I need that intimate relationship with her. I need her touch. I need her scent. I need to hear her voice. I need that part of our relationship.

It's almost like an experience that we have together. Sex makes me feel regular. It helps my body and mind stay normal. Sex between my wife and I keeps me happy.

Now, let's talk about how *"My Need"* can affect my relationship in the sex arena. As you can see, I believe sex is important for marriages, right? Right! So when I don't get it, things change. I get all uptight, short with people, and extra touchy. I might pop off at the mouth for no reason; just unfriendly. In these moments of no physical interaction between my wife and me, I can become vulnerable and open to sin. *Vulnerable to what?* You may be asking. To the other woman. I have developed the need for love and conversation that only a woman could give me. Things that I should only be seeking from my spouse.

In relationships it's vital to know your mate, but it's also necessary that you know yourself. Know what opens the doors to yourself so that you don't allow anyone to knock on your door of life and then invade your life with problems.

I'll show you how being vulnerable could open the door to the enemy in my life.

Let's use this scenario. Imagine me being at work or church, or somewhere else by myself and this pretty woman comes over and begins to talk to me, and I begin to talk back to her. So here we are just talking away. In a time frame of maybe 15 minutes, we find out that we have something in common, and we make a connection.

Are we both wrong? – *Yes.* Should we stop talking? – *Of course.* Do we? – *No.* Why? – *Because I'm not thinking regularly. I'm not focused, and my walls aren't as high as they usually are.*

As time goes by, we both begin to catch feelings, even though we tell each other not to, we still do. So as we both catch these feelings, more feelings come and then we want to become more. And once we want to become more, sex is discussed because that's the only thing left to do. We believe we **need it** to make our relationship complete.

In doing so, we will fill a hidden desire we both need called *companionship*.

Companionship by definition is a feeling one gets in the presence of a companion. The feeling one gets in fellowship or friendship.

Companionship is a real feeling that we all have.

Throughout our lives, we will have moments of feelings with certain people that we can't describe. All we know is that when we're around them, this indescribable feeling is felt. I call that feeling Companionship. You can find happiness, completion, involvement, and peace when in the presence of your companion.

Don't get this word confused with the name of Jesus, where everything you will ever need is found and where every other name shall bow.

I'm talking about that feeling that can be found between two individuals; the feeling that our bodies crave and yearn for. Many times in relationships people exchange their vows, bodies, and promises for companionship, not knowing that they could have kept their vows, body, and promises for their mates and not gave them to someone else.

One key to unlocking your mate is knowing just how badly they may need something, and how important it is for you to give it to them and not someone else. I'm not telling you to be a sex slave. Keep it simple. Simply communicate your need to each other and their importance to each of you. Don't be judgmental or overlook their need because of the size of it or because that's not your need. Remember their need might not be yours, but is just as important, equal, and significant as yours.

Here are simple Suggestions you can try:

1. Simple daily or weekly compliments.

2. Simple touches and rubs can mean a lot and defuse an angry spirit.

3. Simply ask, "What can I do to make you feel better?"

Here is something to beware of:

- Developing a *companionship* with the wrong person can easily be confusing because it feels so real that it can make you believe it's the right thing to do.

Here is something do:

- Self-check yourself regularly by asking yourself *who* is someone you know that can give you this feeling?

Here is something I've learned:

- Sin can be like soda. It's not good for you, yet it taste good and can give your body energy while harming you at the same time.

- What is something that gives you energy or brings you alive that isn't good for you?

Greed

- **Greed** by definition is an *inordinate or rapacious* longing for wealth, desire for possessing or having more than one needs.

When someone is in need, they are mentally vulnerable. But if they are in greed, they will never feel complete no matter how many people they sleep with or how much money they make. Greed can never be satisfied.

For example, during Robyn's high school and college years, Robyn received a lot of attention because of her looks. She wouldn't do anything special to receive this attention, it just happened. Guys would send messages to her by their friends, while some would walk up to her to say what's up, pretty much anything they could do to grab her attention and acknowledge her beauty. Because of the attention she received, she developed a desire for attention. She liked the way it made her feel. She liked that it set her apart from other girls. She even began to expect guys notice her everywhere she went, which usually happened. Even when she had a boyfriend, she would still expect and desire attention from other guys.

Note to self: Don't allow greed to influence you to the place where you feel and believe you need more of something when you already have the thing you desire.

This is a prime example of greed. Robyn told me she wanted

compliments like, "Hey girl, can I get with you?" or "You need to be with me 'cause you so fine." Or my favorite, "Is there any more room for me in those jeans?" (Remember that song?)

Robyn developed the desire to be the center of attention. Even when she had me ☹ as her boyfriend who was giving her all of that attention anyone could have she believed she needed more. Hidden behind her need was greed. Her greed almost cost our relationship.

She didn't "need" the attention. She liked it. She wasn't missing out on any attention. She had it. But because of the desire she had within herself the attention she was getting, wasn't enough. She would always want more. She became greedy. This greed began to hurt her relationships in the way that no matter what I would do, it wouldn't be enough. She always wanted more. In greed, the cup can never be filled. There is not a cup big enough to fill a greedy person's "need."

The only way to fix the greed is to admit to it. "Own it" so that you can let it go. That's what Robyn and I had to do. She had to notice that she was being greedy. She had to realize through our talking and praying that she was greedy. God opened her eyes. She now feels bad when she gets extra attention because her beauty hasn't gone anywhere.

The moral of the story is: Greed can make you feel that you're missing out in life if you don't have enough money, friends, clothes, etc. Make sure that you are attentive to your mate's personality. Needs HAVE to be met, and greed MUST be dealt with within a relationship for a couple to have the relationship God intended for them to have.

So talk it over with each other. Discuss the things that you both have noticed about each other. Don't ignore them. Don't allow the need or greed in your mate to kill your relationship because you allowed yourself to believe "it'll be alright, just give it time." Don't make yourself ignore or cover up a door that needs to be unlocked and opened; a door that only you as that person's life long spouse and friend can unlock.

-Open Ses a me

Distracted

I believe we all can agree that it's easy for us as people to get distracted.

Distracted by definition means *to be mentally confused, troubled, or remote.*

Remote- means to be separated by an interval or space greater than the usual.

In this chapter, I'm going to tell you a funny but serious scenario about how visible doors in relationships can become hidden.

The following pictures are simple examples of what can happen in a relationship when we become distracted by our perceptions.

Staring:

> **Me** ------the bound man in the chair, trying to explain something personal to his wife.

Robyn

The supportive and loving spouse.

And These Two: The **Distraction** & **The Struggle**

Some Lady     The One

Home Sweet Home

Home Sweet Home

Home Sweet Home

This can easily happen in any relationship. Where you may have one person trying to explain themselves and their actions to their mate but their mate hears something else. Or, one mate is saying one thing while their mate has already come up with the answer and has already made up their mind on what to believe. What I would like to shine a light on is that sometimes the thing we tend to see as a threat isn't always the thing we should be worried about. The first thing we see distracts us, but usually, it's what we can't see that is the real threat.

When we say things like *I bet that's it, I know it is*! We're clearly not paying our mate any attention because we *already know*. We see someone or something and tells ourselves *that's the threat right there*. So when the thing we were focusing on is gone, the thing we should have been focusing on "pops up" and we're like, "Where did this come from?"

Problems like these stay hidden because:

1. We don't listen to the person that was talking to us.
2. We don't believe the person talking knows what they were talking about.
3. Or we think we know better than the person talking to us.

Distractions can come from anywhere and to all walks of life. Our job in our relationships is not to get distracted by things that don't even matter or things that are not real threats.

When someone close to you is saying, "Listen to me," they may mean it. When someone close to you says, "Hey I need you to believe me on this," try to trust their judgment. I want to encourage you to support each other in the areas that you're the most bound or vulnerable. It takes two to tango, but it only takes one to leave the post and jeopardize everything.

Don't get distracted.

Pride and Ego

The goal for this chapter is to help both men and women distinguish the difference between Godly Pride and Ungodly Pride & Ego and an Egoist. I believe that it is necessary that all couples know that there is a line between pride and ego that should not be crossed by either party.

As far back as I can remember, my dad always expected me to do my best in everything that I did. He didn't expect me to be perfect, but he did expect me to do well at whatever it was that I was doing and for me to do it right. It didn't matter if I was cooking, cleaning or fixing something. I was always expected to do it right and complete the job. I can remember him first showing me what to do, then telling me how to, and then expecting me to do the same thing that he had done. My dad would also tell me that once I knew what I was doing, I could put my own touch to it as long as I did it right.

Growing up, I would watch my dad do, what seemed to me, everything. I watched the way he took care of my mom, his mom, and my sister, and whoever else needed help. I also paid attention to how people reacted to the things he did for them and how much they appreciated him for it. I could tell that my dad took pride in whatever he did.

Pride *can be defined as a reasonable self-respect based on a consciousness of worth; that which causes one to be proud.*

So as a young boy growing into a young man that has grown into the man I am today, I too take pride in almost everything that I do. I'm not saying that I hit the mark of perfection, but I do try my best to complete the job and do it well.

I'm a firm believer that men and women see pride totally different. Is pride a bad thing? Only when it is **Ungodly Pride**. The Bible explains in –

- **Proverbs 29:23 A man's pride shall bring him low: but honor shall uphold the humble in spirit.**

- **Proverbs 11:2 *When* pride cometh, then cometh shame: but with the lowly *is* wisdom.**

- **Proverbs 14:3 In the mouth of the foolish *is* a rod of pride: but the lips of the wise shall preserve them.**

These are all examples of ungodly pride and how this type of pride can ruin a man's relationship with a woman, his family, and his belongings. However, the kind of pride that I would like to focus on is the pride that makes up the man.

Taking Pride in a Thing

Accomplishments, achievements, and past victories all build a man's pride. His family life, a faithful wife, as well as his kids all can make a man proud.

And when a man has something to be proud of, he sub-consciously takes pride in taking care of it. Over time, by him being proud of the things important to him, his ego is built up.

Ego can be defined by a person's self-esteem or self-importance. (Which is a good thing.)

That being said, are you beginning to see the differences between pride and ego? Pride and ego are usually taken out of context, but they also can be kept in context and used for good. Someone can have a sense of Godly pride where they can focus on God and what He has blessed them with. Or someone can have a sense of Ungodly pride where they focus on themselves, and what they have, or what they have done.

Unfortunately on the other side of Ego there is a person who can be called an **egoist** (aka Big Ego), which is a self-centered, selfish, and often is arrogant and conceited. An egoist is what most people are referring to when they see a man or woman that is all about themselves. This type of person is usually talking up themselves and making a big deal out of what they have going for them and how they are such a blessing to their world.

Let's look back at ego. A man doesn't need a woman to "technically" stroke his ego. What he need is supportive and loving words from his wife. To stroke someone's ego is basically just tell someone what they want to hear to make them feel good whether it is true or not and no one needs that. I believe all human beings need supportive love; we just don't need to be buttered up, flattered, and polished up to believe in something that is not true about ourselves. We owe it to our mates to be honest, open and understanding. When it comes to Pride and Ego find the line that separates the two and keep clear from it, because if you don't, you may find the thin line between love and hate.

Foundations

> "Therefore whoever hears these sayings of mine, and does them, I will liken him to a wise man who built his house on the rock
> **Matt 7:24 (NKJV)**

In the beginning of our marriage, Robyn and I built our marriage on sex, kids, careers, church, and had Jesus as our covering. Sounds like the perfect house, right?

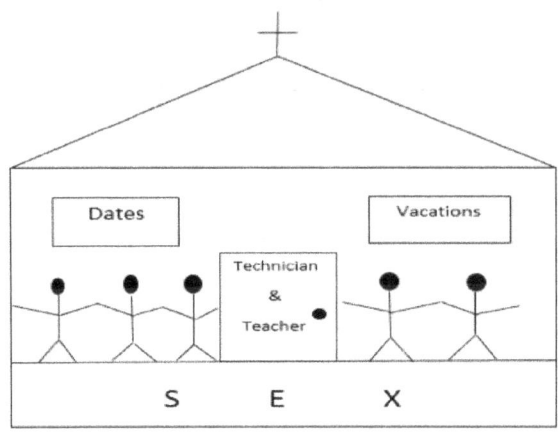

This is not the way a house of endurance should look. But unfortunately, this was the way Robyn and I had built our home. The Bible says in Matt 7:26-27 KJV,

> **"And every one that heareth these sayings of mine, and doeth them not, shall be likened unto a foolish man, which built his house upon the sand: And the rain descended, and the floods came, and the winds blew, and beat upon that house; and it fell: and great was the fall of it."**

This verse is referring to what happens to us when we don't build our house on a strong foundation. Since Robyn and I built our house on sex, kids, careers, church and then Jesus, when the bills began raining down on us and people from our past popped up like a flood, with untold stories like what happened to Zeke, the Freak in the movie, "Think Like a Man II," and secrets just so happened to blow in like the wind, our house began to sway. The Bible says in verse 27 that your house will fall and when it falls it will be a great fall.

This can be encountered through social media.

We encountered a lot of damage to our marriage. Our trust was damaged. We got offended at each other. Instead of looking to each other for support, we looked to our friends and relatives for support. Like always, God got our attention one Sunday in service and saved us by turning our way of doing things into His way.

He taught us to be like the wise man described in Matt

7:24-25(NLT).

> **Anyone who listens to my teaching and follows it is wise, like a person who builds a house on solid rock.** [25] **Though the rain comes in torrents and the floodwaters rise and the winds beat against that house, it won't collapse because it is built on bedrock.**
> Matt 7:24-25 (NLT)

I want to encourage you to want to have a strong house that is built on a solid foundation. The following picture displays the house Robyn and I are using now.

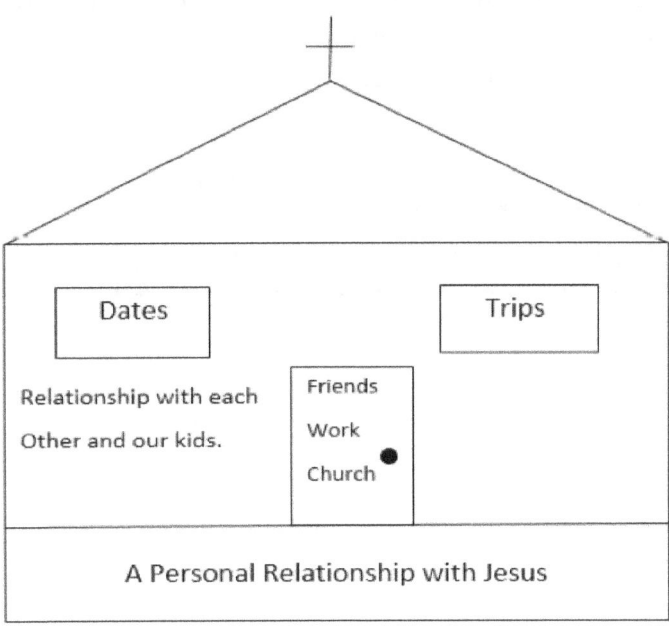

Living in the times that we're in now, I believe we all should have our relationships on a solid foundation. We should prioritize our lives by making sure we have a solid foundation. I want to encourage you that if your foundation is working continue to do routine checks-ups like going on dates and vacations to make sure your foundation has no cracks.

God did it for Robyn and I, and I believe that He will do it for you as long as you don't give up, and see that having a strong foundation as a necessity.

Build a house with worth living in and have great sex in it.

Unlocking   *Foundations*

Activity for you and your mate:

Using the following pictures, fill in what best describes the house you have now.

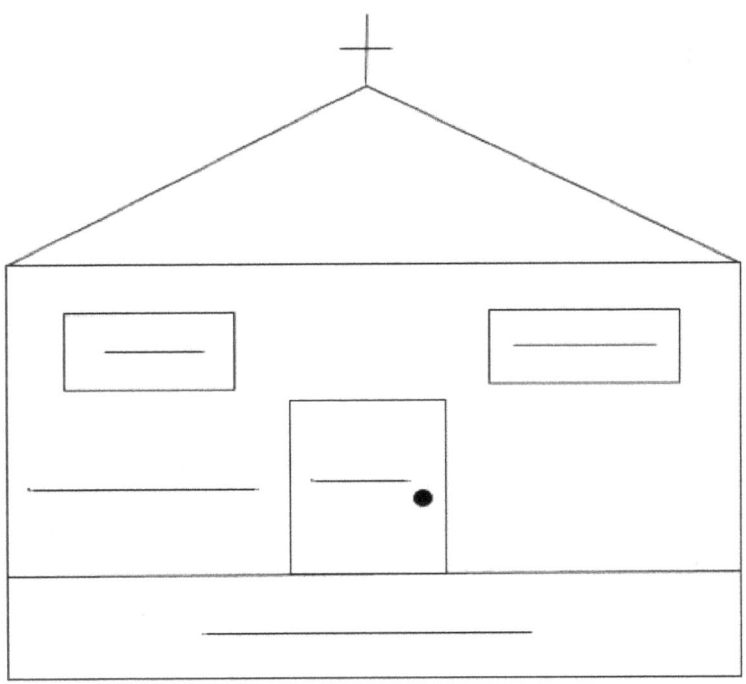

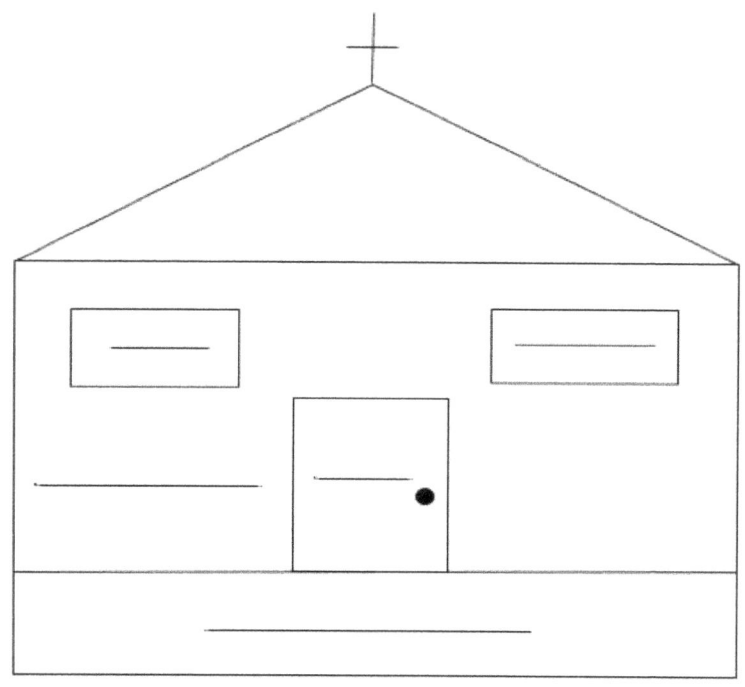

Now, if there's room for improvement, fill in how you would like your house to be built or how you believe a house of endurance should be built so that when the rains, floods, and winds of life come, your house will stand.

Unlocking   *Foundations*

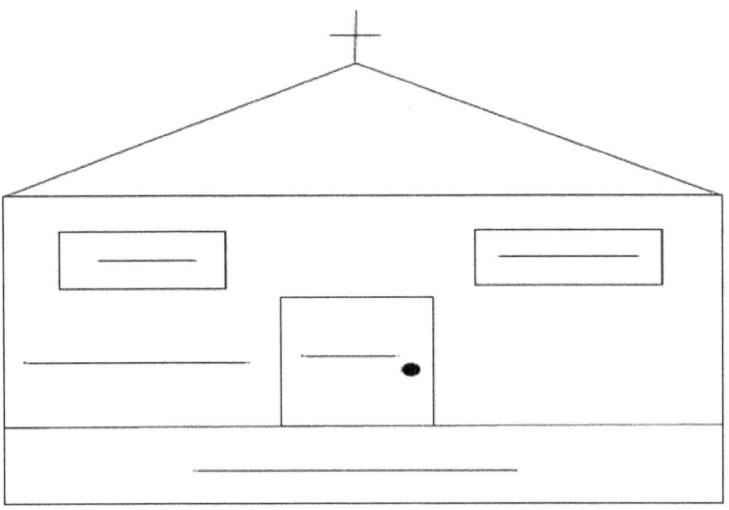

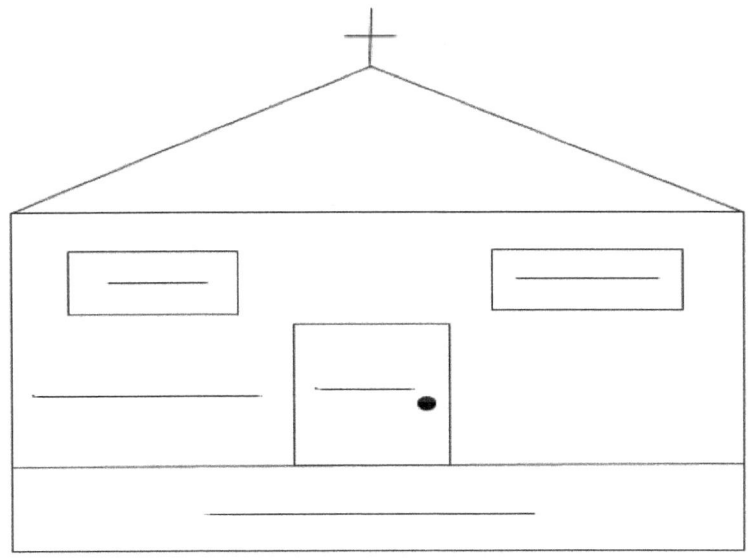

Intentions

Intention by definition is a plan, purpose, or goal of carrying out an action or actions in the future.

The intent of this chapter is to warn couples of hidden intentions that sometimes get overlooked because someone either covered-up or kept important information from their mate.
 Its human nature to keep embarrassing, unusual, and tempting thoughts to ourselves. As the old saying goes, "Some things are just better off unsaid." In a relationship, it's easy to keep personal things from each other for fear of being misunderstood or someone overreacting, which makes it seem easier to just not say anything at all.

There have been times when I saw someone from my past and knew that if I told Robyn, she would either bug out or get down and out. There have also been times when Robyn saw someone from her past and didn't tell me because she knew I would bug out and question her. Since we both worked at different places, she knew people that I didn't know, and I knew people that she didn't know. We talked about them in conversations, but neither of us *really* knew them.

We never knew how the other one really acted around their friends. Robyn and I had appropriate and inappropriate conversations with our associates because of our work settings. But due to immaturity, need, loneliness, greed and many other things within us, we allowed things to be hidden from each other that we shouldn't have, putting ourselves in avoidable positions. After disagreements, long talks at night, and giving each other the cold shoulder, we had to come up with something. Our key was to say, "Hey, I saw _____ the other day."

I want to encourage you to be up front and truthful to one another early in your relationship and don't develop the habit of keeping things hidden in your marriage. The more you do it, the easier it gets, the more junk you will have hidden from your mate. Keep the "youth" in your marriage. Don't allow it to get old and stale, but mature and adventurous.

Get use to the idea of withholding nothing from each other **early** because sin grows in darkness. You will be amazed at how much better you'll feel and how much healthier your relationship will be, because of the openness in your relationship. Talk with openness, fulfillment, purpose and joy.

Wrong Intentions

Now let's shift gears and take a look at this picture or scenario involving two people with what could be four different intentions.

- # 1- The elderly man has the intention of getting help from someone that can help him.

- #2- The elderly man has the intention of taking a peek at what his nurse is working with by having her bend over to "pick something up" that he has so conveniently "dropped."

- #3- The attractive nurse has the intention of teasing the elderly man by showing off her body with revealing clothes and bouncing around in front of him.

- #4- The attractive nurse has the intention of getting her job done in a professional manner and enjoys helping her patients.

Have you ever played any of these roles? Were you like the old man who the excuse of being sick to have someone wait on him, when in truth he was fine and really didn't need anyone to help him? Have you ever been like the lady and used your good looks to get what you wanted without asking, or to tease someone just because you like the attention it brings?

There are many ways we can view and explain our intentions, but we must be mindful of is how it affects our mate and those around us. To me it's all good if you're single and have no responsibility. But if you're married or in a relationship with someone, and you do this kind of stuff for fun, you have to be aware that everyone may not see it the way you do.

Our Intentions

For some people, practical jokes and pranks are just used for fun. But as the old saying goes, "It's all fun and games until someone gets hurt." In this chapter I want to shine light on the *uh-oh's*, the *my bads*, the *I'm sorries*, and the *I didn't knows*, that can slowly rip a relationship apart over time.

Can you think back to a time in your life when you "played" someone in order to get something you wanted? They trusted you because they thought you were trustworthy, only to find out that you weren't. Has there ever been a time when, in certain situations, you could have made better choices, but you didn't *really* know what you were doing? You knew you were doing something, but you didn't really know that the thing you were doing would cause someone else to have a provocative thought. I know that I wouldn't want Robyn bending over in front other men or eating a banana in front of men causing those men to have sexual thoughts. I know Robyn wouldn't like me to hug or put my arm around another woman's waist or tell her a joke that would make Robyn look bad and put that woman in the position of thinking she could do a better job for me as a wife than Robyn could.

My goal here is to help couples avoid problems that are hidden behind doors that we usually don't see until it's too late. I don't want to discourage you from having fun, but I want to make you aware of your actions and the perception of your actions of by those closest to you. Take for instance how a husband may feel if his wife wears clothes that may be (to him) too tight or revealing. She may think that the clothes look good on her, and they probably do, but what she doesn't know is how her husband is *really* feeling and what he is *really* thinking on the inside. She may know that he prefers for her not to wear certain outfits, but she doesn't know that to him, her clothes are tearing their marriage apart and she can't even see it. She doesn't know that her hidden intentions are causing him to have hidden questions about her clothing. He may be wondering, "*Who is she trying to impress? She looks better out there than she does here. We've been together all this time and she still doesn't have a clue about how I really feel. I know that she doesn't know because she hasn't been paying me enough attention to see that when she does this, I do that.*" That's a problem that must be fixed. She knows something, but she *really* doesn't have a clue.

On the flip side of that coin, take a man that likes to make jokes about his wife or his girlfriend in front of people. He may see her laughing with the crowd, but in the back of her mind she is *really* thinking, "*I really wish he would stop doing this because it's embarrassing, especially in front of female friends that I already feel insecure around because* they do everything that I don't know how to do. *This makes feel like I am not a good enough wife for him.*"-

I'm sure both partners have talked with each other a time or two about this, but they haven't stopped yet.

Hidden intentions are all fun and games until someone gets hurt or worse, divorced because someone tolerated_____ for so long and kept it hidden.

Then one day they just pop up and say, "I'm done," walking away from everything that really matters because their feelings and emotions didn't seem to matter enough to the other person for them to *Stop*.

We could go on and on about situations that could have been prevented if only we paid enough attention to what was really going on around us and with others. Let's be mindful of our intentions. We may be intending one thing but someone else may be seeing something else.

Reveal your intentions to your mate. Explain to them why you like certain things, whether it's clothes, friends, foods, places, or certain environments. Whatever it is, allow your mate to be able to look into the person you are and be intimate with that person.

-God Bless

The Boxing Ring

What every fighting man wants.

I want to start off explaining what a fighting man is to me. I believe a fighting man is ANYONE that is fighting for the betterment of his family, himself, and those he knows because of the call on his life. Please understand I'm not talking about those that serve our country. I believe that there's no Greater Call than to lay down your life for another. I'm coming from a small scale, but a scale that is just as important. The fighting man I'm relating to is similar to the man Paul talks about in 2 Timothy 2:3.

Endure suffering along with me, as a good soldier of Christ Jesus. 2 Timothy 2:3 (NLT)

I want to share my view as a fighting man because I know from experience that there are other fighting people out there, but we're hard to recognize because:

- We don't talk a lot.

- We don't have large groups of friends even though we

know a lot of people.
- We keep to ourselves because we don't like extra distractions.

The fighting man I'm referring to sees and believes in things other people don't. Everyone won't relate to this but this relates me. One thing I've learned is this: I can't change what is true to you, just like you can't change what is true to me. We must get passed our beliefs in order to truly listen to someone to see how they see. Once we're able to get on their level, we'll be able to understand where their coming from.

"People don't care how much you know until they know how much you care."
–John C. Maxwell.

As a man fighting to do the right thing for what I call My Life in Christ, Robyn and I had some challenges of our own.

Looking back on my relationship with Robyn, I can remember her coming up to me as my girlfriend asking me, "Ben, what do you need from me?" At that time I can remember responding to her saying, "Babe, all I need is you to be you."

Back then that's all I needed. I felt empowered knowing I had a beautiful woman in my life.

Sounds sweet doesn't it? Two people flourishing in love, on fire for the Lord, and ready to conquer the world together.

Now let's fast-forward to the married life.

Unlocking   *The Fighter*

After being married for some years now, I see life differently. As a man fighting to do his best for his family and for himself, I can now see what I really need from my wife. Picture this: me against the world, with my wife in one corner and God in the other. God telling me what to do and my wife there for reassuring support.

In my book, The Making, I described the importance of two people being there for each other from the position of them *walking* through life together. In this book, I'm describing the importance of two people *standing their ground* together when it seems to be them against the world.

Robyn and I realized the importance of togetherness after losing major fights due to our separate expectations. So speaking from a fighting man's point of view, here is a picture of how our marriage looked during my fight against the world.

One of the things I realized was that I didn't need a judge. I didn't need a woman that would just sit back in the crowd and watch me like everyone else. I needed support. I didn't need to be viewed as a man that couldn't. I needed a woman that could bite her tongue long enough for me to get up and get back into the fight without her saying anything negative.

I believe every fighting man needs a woman who has a sensitive relationship with God. One that can hear from Him on her own and respect His actions as her husband's coach who has been training him on how to fight the Lord's fight. A woman that can be in his corner so that when the round is over, he can come to her and she is able to stomach the look of a man that has been hurt or the look of a man that has messed up in life.

A fighting man needs a woman that pays him enough attention to learn his habits and patterns. He needs a woman that can watch him fight and can tell him things like, "You keep getting hit because you keep dropping your right. Hold it up and you'll block it every time." He needs a woman that can wipe the sweat and blood off his face and say, "I'm proud of you, now get back out there."

Unfortunately, Robyn and I didn't start our marriage like this. In the beginning I thought I was supposed to do everything on my own. You know, how the world told us to believe. Do everything and accomplish nothing. I thought I was supposed to be Superman, "Here to save the day!" And by believing that, I crippled Robyn's potential to be a better wife for me. I sat her on the sidelines with the crowd while I did everything.

By me keeping her from doing anything, she became complacent. By her becoming complacent, she became settled, and by her being settled, she felt unneeded. By her feeling unneeded, she believed she was unwanted, and no one wants to feel that way.

The only thing Robyn saw was me trying to do what God told me to do. She thought her lot in life was to simply cheer me on and tell me that, "*If you think that's best thing to do, do it.*" She believed that by doing those things, she was being a supportive wife. And really, in the boyfriend-girlfriend stage of our relationship that was what I told her I needed her to be. But now, being married with responsibilities like kids, bills, and each other, we've had to become aware of how to handle our roles in our relationship.

Men, if I were you, I would go over these two scenarios and see if they relate to you. Whether they do or don't, talk it over with your wife and tell her what you need. I understand that some men may not want their wives that close to the action and prefer them to be in the crowd as a trophy wife or cheerleader. Some men may want their wives to be the pretty woman that announces the beginning of each round. I believe, whatever the case may be, we as men should open the door to our arena of life and allow our wives to be our help and fulfill the need we have.

Women, I know that this may be a lot to ask of you. That's why I believe it's important for women to have a real, genuine relationship with God because what a fighting man needs, the average woman can't give without God's help.

Let me encourage you to stay in the fight together. My wife and I like to see people win. So many people we know have lost out in life because they didn't understand how, know how, or want to act as a team when it came to fighting together in marriage. They lost out on so much just because one person was in the wrong post in life and separated in divorce or just shut down and decided to give up. We understand it's hard on both individuals in a relationship. We completely understand that because we're nowhere near perfect ourselves. I understand the man that gets physically beat down while the woman is getting emotionally and mentally beat down from watching her man fight for what he believes. The fight can take a toll on both people. We all have to realize that one position isn't better than the other. Robyn and I want you to win. We all must continue to fight the good fight of faith and conquer our lives together, one swing at a time. It's not easy, but it's worth it.

Assignment Time

I want to leave you with this thought/question:
Who's more important? Jesus or God's people? You can't

have one without the other.

Explain your answer and talk it over with one another. (Without fussing please.)

Define what you are fighting for, what you will have to fight for or why you are fighting.
-And fight on.

The Dog

In this chapter, I will give you a personal scenario between Robyn, a dog, and me, and how we ran into a locked door because of our thinking. It opened our eyes to the importance of having a plan, which is the key we needed to get through a hidden door of the "unexpected" so that we both could react in the same manner in what seemed to be a threatening environment.

About six years ago, we were outside playing with our kids and one of my neighbor's dogs got loose. It was a house pet, so it wasn't an aggressive dog, but to my little kids who were afraid of dogs, it didn't matter what kind of dog it was. They just knew that it was a dog and it was chasing them. I was on the road teaching one of my daughters how to ride a bike without training wheels when the dog ran into our yard, so I couldn't just drop her and chase the dog off. The dog ran around my son trying to get him to play, but my son freaked out.

Robyn was holding our baby girl while watching the other kids play in the front yard, so I yelled to Robyn, "Get the boy. Pick him up." But all she did was say, "Get dog… get," trying to shoo the dog off.

That wasn't working so I shouted, "What are you doing, get the boy!" And she yelled back, "I am Ben," shouting at the dog again, "Get dog! Get!" So there we were freaking out over this dog that wanted to play with us. Our kids were bugging out because of us freaking out; all over nothing.

I picked my daughter up, ran after the dog, picked my son up and said, "Everybody go in the house!" Being hyped up from the moment, I told Robyn, "Whenever someone is in trouble, you pick them up and carry them to safety!" Robyn's reply was, "My way of protecting people is to keep them away from any possibility of threat from the start. I attack the threat before it has a chance to attack me. That's why I tried to shoo the dog off."

Freeze: Who was right? I was taught to snatch a person up if they're in trouble, but Robyn was taught to be on guard of anything that can cause trouble. Little hidden doors of different expectations and miscommunication like these can turn the strongest couple against one another in a moment if not handled correctly.

Unfreeze: My son was fine, but Robyn and I were so worked up about how bad we worked against each other in that moment that we couldn't understand what had happened. If that had been a real situation with a bad dog, things could have been a lot worse.

That moment created an eye-opening lesson between the two of us. Growing up my parents allowed me to venture off and learn things, causing me to use my common sense. They also taught me how to get back home if I needed anything or got into trouble. Robyn's folks protected her from trouble by covering her. They looked at certain situations and thought that it would be best for her not to do certain things.

Robyn and I believe that we learned great parenting skills from our parents, and we needed to combine our differences together to teach our children.-Going off our own experiences without a plan wasn't enough. We had never talked about what we would do if a dog ran into our yard. Hidden inside of us was truth but we never thought to open the door to see what was inside.

Have you ever thought about how you would rescue someone you know from trouble? Have you ever wondered how your mate may act in a "what if" moment? I believe we all have different ways of doing things, but trouble and sin are two things that need to be handled quickly. We all need to have a plan of action to save and protect ourselves and those closest to us.

You need a plan if your mate goes off the deep end, and your mate needs a plan if you go off the deep end. I would suggest that you and your mate, or your mate to be, develop a plan so that you both can be on the same page when trouble comes. A dog may not run into your yard, but something else may hit close to home. That's why it's best to have a plan.

If someone you know is in trouble, you and your mate can save the day together with an organized plan. In a situation like ours, we both had good plans; we just weren't on the same page.

-Have a plan or plan to lose.

The "Thought-of" Effect

The Face behind the Mask of Fear

Have you ever missed out on something you wanted to do just because you had a ***thought*** that stopped you from doing it? But now looking back at the whole situation you can see how only if you would have continued you would have been able to do it.

This is what I want to go over in this chapter. There are things hidden within us we have something that only pops up when we're about to make a decision to do something that can be of benefit to us.

I want couples to know that if we allow whatever it is to stay hidden, we will not fulfill the true purpose of our relationship. We will stay on the sidelines of life watching everyone around us move further on in life.

As a couple, we should want our mates to win in the things they like to do. But for us to win, we have to ask each other questions like:

Unlocking   *The Thought-of*

- What is something that can make you shutdown right before you make a big decision?

- What something that can discourage you to the place of Throwing in the Towel before the game even starts?

Couples must learn how to keep each other accountable, but at the same time be mindful of how their mate feel about the situation.

One way of doing this is to tell each other your plan of action, including the emotions that you both had before you act. Robyn and I have come to find out that its best for us to document everything that is happening with us during the time of preparation so that when it's time for action neither one of us will turn back or have a change of heart that will cause us to

---

Then the LORD answered me and said: "Write the vision. And make it plain on tablets, that he may run who reads it. Habakkuk 2:2 (NKJV)

---

forfeit our future due to a ***thought***.

In doing this, you will be keeping each other accountable, because once you act, things are going to change and you may not want to finish what you started. One person may want to quit and the other may want to continue. One person may be willing to get married; have kids; or quit their job and pursue something better. The list can go on and on about opportunities missed just because someone had a ***thought*** that made them change their mind.

The *"thought-of"* goes deeper than just being afraid of dogs, snakes, bugs or flying in a plane. It can go as deep as believing you may lose something or someone that is dear to us. The *thought-of* is more than the average doubt or fear of death or divorce. It's more like thinking, "*If this doesn't go through I am going to lose everything."* The *thought-of effect* deals with situations that hopefully won't happen, but have a chance of happening, mainly dealing with you and your future.

The *thought-of effect* has kept me up night after night. I can remember waking up at 2:00 in the morning just thinking about what happen or what might happen. I'm not just talking about what some people call the Spirit of Fear. I'm talking about the thing that causes you to lose your appetite. It can make your face flush and your heart to skip a beat. It can be the Deal Breaker.

The *thought-of effect* is a real thing, and everyone may not deal with it depending on his or her level of maturity or belief. Usually, one of the people in the relationship deals with it, and they need someone to be there with them to help them handle it.

The *thought-of effect* is an extreme case of the unknown. Unknown thoughts of what may happen and what could happen. When the *thought-of* is affecting us, we don't have thoughts-of what **should** happen so much as what **would** happen. We only have negative thoughts that lead to other negative thoughts. The *thought-of* can affect you in a very powerful way if you allow it.

Here are some recommendations to do so that you won't keep this door closed in your life:

1. Acknowledge to yourself that there is a possible problem present.

2. Acknowledge to your mate (if it's something concerning them or concerns both of you) that there is a problem present and you need to talk it all the way through with them. This way you can have a plan of action if something were to go wrong or turned out the way you feared it to.

3. Tell God about it. Pray and ask Him for strength.

I recommend that you do all three as a whole, and not as steps, because sometimes when we only tell God about it. That's as far as it goes. We believe that as long as we told Him, that's all we need to do.

My friend, I want to remind you that He made us to be in relationships and to have fellowship with others. Be encouraged and know that you can overcome the thought-of effect because your more than a conquer. You can enjoy life with those closest to you.

Fear not and know God is with you.

Imaginary Problems

In the beginning of my marriage, I was the king of having imaginary problems in my marriage. I was that guy. I was what most people called suspicious of just about anything and everything. Robyn couldn't tell because I would often play it off. But in the back of my mind, I was like the guy spying from behind a bush. I knew what I had, and I didn't want to lose it.

Am I proud of it? No. Is it ok to be like that? No! Am I alone? No! There are other people out there in Relationship Land, just like me, who have insecurities that can turn their insecurities into imaginary problems.

Imaginary problems come from not knowing the outcome of your future when odds are, or may look to be, against you. Sometimes bad experiences can create imaginary problems that cause us not to act, trust, and believe for a better future.

Hidden imaginary problems can ruin a healthy relationship, mainly when there's nothing going on and one of the two begins to accuse the other of something due to a feeling or a thought.

So what does one do? The key is open communication and prayer. Prayer will hopefully calm you down and ease your stress long enough for the two of you to talk about your fear of what's going on and why. Then open communication will open your eyes to the truth of what is really going on around and within you. Don't allow imaginary problems to keep your fear hidden and your relationships on the edge of breaking up due imaginary problems. Spend time talking with your mate and thinking to yourself on the hidden fears within you.

Hidden Fears

For God hath not given us the spirit of fear; but of power, and of love, and of a sound mind. 2 Timothy 1:7 KJV

A spirit of fear can be given to us from an outside source, such as the news, negative people, or something worst "The devil". The devil is real folks, but not powerful. All he can do is make suggestions and give immoral ideas. We have the power to cast down and disregard evil thoughts when they come into our mind by speaking and believing in truth and not amplifying or believing those thoughts so that we don't create our own fear in our lives.

Just like love, fear – when allowed – can grow into a heck of an emotion. The Bible says in 1John 4:18 in the Amplified version that:

There is no fear in Love [dread does not exist], but full-grown (complete, perfect) love turns fear out the doors and expels every trace of terror! For fear brings **with it** the *thought* *of* **punishment, and [so] he who is afraid has not reached the** full maturity **of love [is not** yet **grown into love's** complete **perfection].**

Love has different stages. This verse shines a light on how love can be full-grown and mature, meaning this kind of love "casteth out all fear."

I've asked myself the question, *"What do you do if you don't have such fully grown love as the Bible says? What do you do when fear rears its ugly head in your life?"*

Hidden fears have to be confronted. We can't allow hidden fears to stay hidden and kept away in the back of our minds. We cannot make light of hidden fears. We must address the issues and shine light on them in order for us to expel every trace of terror, and not allow the devil to live in the shadows of our fear.

Don't expect you and your mate to get over imaginary problems at the same time. You must stand with each other and help one another get over the hidden fears so that you both can stay a couple.

Face to Face

I can remember riding back home one night after having a disagreement with Robyn and talking to God about how I felt my marriage should be going. I had so much anger, frustration, disappointment, and hatred boiling up in me.

"I DON'T TRUST HER," I said to the Lord. I can remember beating my chest as I spoke with the Lord on how I believed she should be acting, and how I believed I deserved a woman I could trust, and since I didn't trust Robyn, we shouldn't be together.

In the middle of that moment, I can remember motioning my right hand from my chest to in front of me as if Robyn was standing there. I pictured myself placing my face on top of Robyn's face and hating her for acting and looking like me.

Freeze: I hated her for "looking like" she was doing something that I would do.

Have you ever looked at someone such as your mate, or your child, or a relative, or friend/co-worker, or even a pastor and judged their actions even though you have committed the same act?

Have you ever disliked or even hated someone for acting like somebody that hurt you or someone you know, to the point that you didn't want anything to do with him or her even though they hadn't done anything to you? They just looked or acted like someone else.

One of the fastest ways to lock someone out your life is to see them for something or someone that they're not.

Unfreeze: In this moment of internal chaos, the Holy Spirit forced me to see what I was doing. When I looked at her, I saw myself.

God was dealing with me on un-forgiveness. He was showing me that I had un-forgiveness hidden in my heart that needed to be opened so my marriage could be healed from it.

Robyn saw me struggling, but I kept it from her. I even went as far as blaming her for how I felt. I can remember the Holy Spirit saying if you don't reveal it won't be healed.

I caught myself saying things like, *"I don't believe you can be around all those guys and not be attracted to any of them."* I couldn't see how she could be faithful to me in the environment she worked in with those types of men.

My heart was locked on believing, "That will never happen to me." So I locked my heart and stored away so Robyn couldn't hurt it. I was just like a kid with a scrapped knee; I kept it hidden and covered, and didn't want anyone to touch it even though I cried for help.

Things won't get better until you face the issue.

The Holy Spirit showed me that I didn't trust myself in certain situations. If I couldn't trust me, Mr. Do Right! I knew I couldn't trust her (Lil Robyn) because I knew better than she did.

The Holy Spirit revealed to me that I was the untrustworthy one. I was the one that fed off of the attention of others. I was the one that would be picking and choosing. I was the one who thought, "If it was me I would be doing _____."

It was me! I didn't believe it! The Lord said, "Yes, it's you."

I believe the Holy Spirit had to step into the midst of my temperament to correct me so I would realize that not everyone is up to any good. Not everyone is looking for ways to cheat. Everyone isn't like you. There are good people out there despite what the television and movies and the Internet expose.

I had to learn to stop placing my face and actions on others, mainly those closest to me if I was to really trust anyone. As a people, we have been guilty of doing this. We stereotype someone and think to ourselves, *"They're up to no good."* In order for us not to judge others for our wrongdoing, we have to repent, release, and relieve them from the un-forgiveness we have towards ourselves.

<u>Repent</u> from judging and condemning others.

<u>Release</u> them from our little box of "I bet you will".

<u>Relieve</u> ourselves from hidden doors of un-forgiveness.

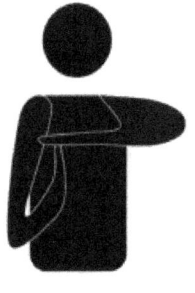

Stop Repenting and Repent

"Stop repenting and repent," the Lord said to me one day while praying. "Stop it!!!" He said, "You're too big. You know too much to continue to act like you don't know. Stop it…" At that time in my life, I was struggling with a situation that had me going back and forth.

Repent by definition is to: *have a change of mind about a past action; to feel sorrow; remorse, or regret for one's past conduct.*

To do, or not to do? Should I go or should I stay? Should I commit or should I recommit? For better or worse, or better for me?

I would go on and on thinking about the pros and cons and dos and don'ts. *What should I do?* I asked myself while complaining to God about how hard it was for me to walk away from the thing I was struggling with and do the right thing.

Freeze: Have you ever seen someone flopping around and screaming for help in the shallow part of a pool, when all they have to do is stand up and they would be fine?

Unfreeze: That's what was going on with me. I wasn't confident enough in myself, so I allowed my surroundings to have more of an influence on me that they should have.

When faced with some of life's challenges, it can be very hard to walk to, through, or away from some of life's tempting mysteries. Thoughts like: I don't know if this opportunity will ever come my way again so *I might as well* just go ahead and do Blank. Or, I only live once so why not Blank?

As a friend and brother in Christ, I want to encourage you to stay strong and focus minded when faced with life's tempting mysteries. One of my goals and purposes for becoming an author and writing books is to warn people of the mistakes that can be made in relationships that have the possibility of setting them back years, or even end healthy relationships that had a chance to thrive and flourish into a godly relationship. I want to enlighten people with material that can help them achieve their own goals in life and have an advantage in their relationship.

Take me for instance; there were times when I had a hard time saying **"No."** I didn't know that I could just Stop. I thought I had to reply to a text message or a missed call. You may be thinking, "Ben, you're a grown man, you should know how to Stop." I agree, but I didn't know. And when people don't know, they don't know, even if we believe they should know, they don't. When a person like me doesn't know what to do, they get into trouble, they do and say things that shouldn't be said. God had to tell me to stop repenting and repent.

If you're not this type of person, but someone that **can** *just* say **"No"** with no problem and no feelings, help someone that can't say no. Please, don't let people take advantage of them. And don't you take advantage of them either. Help them to understand that they have to do what is BEST and not just what is EASY. Sometimes it's easier just to go with it and say yes to whatever that struggle may be even though it may not be God's best for them. If you know how to say no and have someone close to you that doesn't, don't leave them to themselves, but pray for them and with them to encourage and help them to obtain the BEST that God has for them. Show them that they can repent, and they don't have to keep repenting from that same stumbling block.

-Now go ahead and stop.

The Conclusion

As we come to a close, I hope you have found new ways to unlock yourself and mate to be better and stronger people. I hope you have a **Love That Comes First**, so you can **Love them for them** and not get **Distracted** by wrong **Intentions** by **Comparing** them to a **Dog** you once was **Coupled** with after drinking from the wrong **Bottle** that gave you **Imaginary Problems** that made you call **Dr. Fix-it** who said you were full of **Pride** and **Ego** because of your **Need and Greed** for a solid **Foundation** because someone gave you the **Thought-of** having no **Activity** in **The Boxing Ring** in your life. **Stop Repenting** and **Repent** for the sake of your relationship. God has great plans for you, but you can't achieve them alone. We were made to be **Face to Face** in Relationships; therefore, we must learn how **To Be** in a Relationship. I pray and hope that this book has opened you to fresh views that will be a benefit to you and your mate.

With much love and encouragement,

Ben

Message from the Author

As a married man, I would recommend that you and your spouse learn how and continue to work on your relationships in the privacy of your home. What Robyn and I have found out, is that everything works better for us when it is just the two of us wanting to do the right thing by each other for the Will of God for our life.

If you have enjoyed Open Ses·a·me, I recommend that you read my book "The Making." It not only talks about relationship issues, but it also shines a light on having a relationship with God and yourself. I am also pleased to announce my wife's book "Fulfilment." This book is good for moms, teenage daughters, and any woman wanting the "O.K." of being self-fulfilled in who she is, and not the guilt that can come from the world's view of a woman.

I hope you have enjoyed,

Ben.

www.ingramcontent.com/pod-product-compliance
Lightning Source LLC
Chambersburg PA
CBHW070631300426
44113CB00010B/1734